Good
Monster

Also by Diannely Antigua

Ugly Music

Good
Monster

Diannely
Antigua

Copper Canyon Press
Port Townsend, Washington

Copper Canyon Press is in residence at Fort Worden State Park in Port Townsend,
Washington, under the auspices of Centrum. Centrum is a gathering place for
artists and creative thinkers from around the world, students of all ages and
backgrounds, and audiences seeking extraordinary cultural enrichment.

LIBRARY OF CONGRESS CATALOGING-IN-PUBLICATION DATA
Names: Antigua, Diannely, author.
Title: Good monster / Diannely Antigua.
Description: Port Townsend, Washington : Copper Canyon Press, 2024. |
Summary: "A collection of poems by Diannely Antigua"— Provided by publisher.
Identifiers: LCCN 2023052772 (print) | LCCN 2023052773 (ebook) |
ISBN 9781556596902 (paperback) | ISBN 9781619322974 (epub)
Subjects: LCGFT: Poetry.
Classification: LCC PS3601.N56875 G66 2024 (print) |
LCC PS3601.N56875 (ebook) | DDC 811/.6—dc23/eng/20231109
LC record available at https://lccn.loc.gov/2023052772
LC ebook record available at https://lccn.loc.gov/2023052773

9 8 7 6 5 4 3 2 FIRST PRINTING

COPPER CANYON PRESS
Post Office Box 271
Port Townsend, Washington 98368
www.coppercanyonpress.org

for all the monsters

Like when he said I am no good
I am no good
Goodness is not the point anymore
Holding on to things
Now that's the point

Dorothea Lasky, "Ars Poetica"

Contents

Good
Monster

SOMEDAY I'LL STOP KILLING DIANNELY ANTIGUA

This isn't an apology but rather a confession:
I loved your body before I was born.

I counted your future fingers and toes, touched
your hands before they ever touched another's, my left

in your right, and we slept in the womb that exists
before wombs, mouth pressed over mouth,

a position I'd learn to crave.
I loved your body before I was born and

hated your body after my first gasp of rusted air, after
hearing your shriek match my own. Perhaps I hated your body

because of what you could do to another body—
opened it, not a wound but a portal—

and the permission you took
I then took, sixteen years waiting, took a steak knife

to your wrists, drew striped doors,
and the red entered the room.

Once I opened all the pill bottles,
left them on the dresser, watched you—

one, two, three pills at a time—
swallow them in front of the mirror,

reflection slipping into bed after,
into the little trap I'd set. Only twenty minutes

had passed when they found you, strapped
your arms to the gurney,

and I hid under the sheets where I'd held you
moments before, told you the story of Little Red Riding Hood

as you closed your eyes. I'd like to say
I stopped there. A year later I tried it again, ritual

of pills and mirror and bed, and now the story
of the brown babies, all lost before they were lost.

And you wept as I held you once more, understood
this was my task all along, to kill. And what a love to give

in to my violence, your breath weaker, diaphragm
lulled to sleep. How could I not pity you, dear one,

how could I not wipe the spittle from your lips, dial
three numbers. They saved

you again. And you didn't blame me when asked, called
your assassin a name you'd read once in a book about death,

and I thanked you in time,
and in time, I hope to stop trying,

or in time I imagine you'll grow strong,
grab me by the throat, close

a portal perhaps, and I'll forgive you.

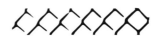

CHRONICALLY

It started at sixteen when instead of falling
in love with Jesus, I fell in love with a boy,
a bit of God's wrath now living
in my right shoulder, right hip,
right side of my newly kissed neck.
I knew he was jealous—God,
not the boy. Instead of Proverbs
before bed, I spoke to the boy
on the phone, whispering, my body
cramped in the dark corner of the living room,
my family already asleep. I told the boy
I loved him, my breathy hallelujah,
like the hush of the MRI machine, taking me
into its mouth, or the X-rays, or my silent
bending over in the blue paper gown,
little ass out in front of the doctor
as he checked my spine. The boy
checked my spine, too, as he reached
under my shirt, unhooked my padded bra.
This was before the diagnosis, the word
itself sounding like a disease, *diagnosis*,
how it shares the first three letters
of my name. *Diagnosis*. If I could take
my tiny shovel hand, carve out
the synapses from my head,
shoulders, knees and toes. Oh bless,
bless, bless, it is meaningless how invisible
the body in pain, when God
is a house I can't leave.

DIARY ENTRY #5: SELF-PORTRAIT AS REVELATIONS

It was the summer of loss spanning the exact distance
disease could reach—the degrees of longitude
and latitude, lonely numbers like decorations
for a forgotten graduation party in a church basement.

The disease reached a longitudinal pain and I
blame the gods of my childhood, Jesus and the TV,
and the basement parties where I became a forgotten church,
when the boys came for pleasure and I asked for mercy.

Jesus just watched TV—sometimes gods can be children.
I had no forgiveness left to play with, alone with my symptoms
of surviving the boys, their pleas for merciful come.
I told myself it was love, when I was a particle suspended

like a plaything, alone and unforgivable. The symptoms
would be permanent, a number registered to the beast.
I tell my unlovable particles the story of how
Little Red Riding Hood went insane after the grandmother

died. Permanence is beastly, all the preparation to live,
all the terrible beauty. What does a teenage girl
know of insanity? It is riding the same red death,
that muddied horse, soaked to a flood.

Maybe I was terrible and beautiful things still happened.
Maybe I was decorated in loneliness, a pretty
death horse muddied by the flood. Maybe I became the flood,
of the spanning summer that took me, lost me.

A HUNDRED AND THEN NONE

Last night a man was yelling in the parking lot as I walked to my car.
I don't know what he said, but it sounded like my name,
like my stepfather when he called me four Christmases ago
from an unknown number, said he loved me like a daughter
as if he'd never touched me like a lover. I was nine. He wasn't
asleep but pretending, his large hairy arms locked around
my frame, my body accustomed only to my mother's hairless arms
in those early years of begging to be close to my creator.
Yesterday the man I'm seeing used the words *love* and *you*
in the same sentence. I can tell summer is coming because I am
afraid. There are pills. Will I be a good mother? I can't forgive her
soft harm. In my family, the women believe in powder under the arms,
under the breasts. Today I hold three pills in my palm
where I once held more than a hundred and then none at all.

SELF-PORTRAIT AS EASTER PAMPHLET ON THE DOOR

There is a special night
a thousand nights from this:

I commemorate my annual dying,
when I witnessed myself as a mountain,

a failed Jehovah, no followers.
I'm trying to reach

the congregation inside me: *Please
join us for the death! You are welcome*

to attend! I'm trying
to remember my giving up:

location, date, and time. Was it
in the meadow by the old school?

Was it April? Were kingdoms
lining the hall to the bathroom,

when on hands and knees
I crawled to the toilet to find

that my cup had not passed, but lived
inside my gut, silver chalice and all?

I forget who witnessed the first time,
who stood in the watchtower on the hill,

placed a Bible at my feet. I'm trying to believe
I'm the collection to be had:

I'm broken like bread.
Take, eat.

I'M SURPRISED AT MY TOLERANCE

for being touched. My thighs
are touched by the plastic chair,
my fingertips touched by the keys, my ass
touched by the swinging door.
At the restaurant, my coworker touches
my shoulder as she passes by to pour
water for her table, only to have my arm
touched by the cold drips from her tray.
I've heard dripping water
can be a torture—the touch, then the
touch, touch of it. When will I stop
the world from touching me?
I'm told to learn boundaries.
What a revolution to say
No.
Sponge, don't touch my elbow
No.
Soap, don't trail down my leg to my feet, to my big toe
No.
Towel, don't dry me
No.
Underwear, don't put your cotton mouth on
No.
I wish I could've said it that day. O little day,
damned day of the unforgettable punishment of touch—
trespass of a nine-year-old body,
his forty-five-year-old grip, how unforgivable
to have his hairy knuckles graze the dimples
on my lower back. Graze as in feed, as in
consume, bushels of dry straw
in a girl's mouth.

PANTOUM IN CASE OF EMERGENCY

Don't call my doctor. Don't call
the neighbor. Maybe I like
to be devastated, to make a medicine
out of neglect. Maybe there is another

neighbor in me who doesn't like
September—another birthday, another year
of neglect, maybe another
day to smell violence in the air. I barely

live till September, another year of birthdays
to stay alive for my eggs, so they can't be used
for violence. To leave their smell in the air, sometimes
I take a spoonful of pills to bed

and see my eggs still alive, never used. Sometimes
I dream of shoving whole loaves of bread into my mouth,
as I spread my worth like pills on the bed. And I can't
stop looking for more bread, even as I spit out

whole dreams shaped like loaves, my whole mouth
open wide to the aisle of the grocery store.
I even stop people to show them my bread spit.
Each time I come back from the hospital,

I open myself wide like an aisle at the grocery store.
I throw away the comforter and paint the walls.
Each time I come back from the hospital,
the deer show up in the parking lot to eat from the bushes.

I throw it all away—my comfort, my walls.
I'm the doctor you didn't call.
I eat the deer. I eat the bushes
to be devastated, to make a medicine.

DIARY ENTRY #13: BEING SICK IS A ROMANTIC IDEA

It was the summer of pain, summer
of becoming the rhythm
of spasms down my cervical spine,
calling it a reunion of ache. I remember
the unbuttoned shirt felt like a grave,
and the grave like practicing the Bible
in a basement, or like being Achilles
in reverse. I was strong
from the ankles down, from my shallow
baptism in the Atlantic. As a child,
I'd heard a story about an angel so beautiful
she was evicted from heaven by the others,
made to live out her days trapped in flesh,
confined to a hospital bed. I'd like to pretend
God called on the phone every day—
a worried Father—or perhaps,
disguised as a nurse, brought her water
and pills. To say I'm not afraid of dying
is to admit I want to be stared at
like something to lose. I thought I could
leave with the dignity any breaking woman
would want. I haven't been sleeping
or walking or kissing the people I love.
Sometimes my lips will graze an ear,
a freshly shaved neck.

CONNECTIONS

Back then, I called him something more
than father. His voice could fill

more than rooms—it could fill the space between
the bedroom, to the kitchen, to my mother, to her face.

It's hard to forget a mouth that's hurt you—white teeth,
gums pink and clean, his lips whistling

for one of us to bring him ice water, my whistle
the catcall whistle, the one he used the most. I forget

my own mouth that August afternoon
while watching TV on his bed. I remember

showering after, his voice at the bathroom door
calling what happened a game. We did play

a game once, the first time I saw the lights
of New York while sitting on his shoulders,

while clinging to his jacket, the windbreaker slipping
through my sweaty little palms. I had to guess

which building was the tallest, each growing
bigger to my eyes, the antennas sticking out the tops

like great insects teaching me how to bow.
When I moved to Brooklyn decades later,

I practiced bowing to the skyline while riding
the M train to Manhattan—the sharp contours

glistening with the dew only metal can perform.
I practiced bowing at the base of the Empire

State Building, midnight on my 26th birthday,
my body feeling just as small as before,

in awe, how dangerous and fleeting this joy,
like a summer day turned trauma. I admit

I love a city that reminds me of him.
I admit something was planted in me, the need

to complicate a happiness. He taught me
that lesson, from a place so high up I don't know

how I'd get there again, how I could possibly touch
the hem of a cloud from here.

DIARY ENTRY #12: THE MONSTER

It was after my 22nd birthday   when a monster rose

     to greet me from the confines   of the basement.

  She was a secret   friend, liked cookies and beer.

      Once, I read her

a book about a boy   who bribed girls in dresses

      to climb coconut trees.

Once, I read her a Sears   catalogue, and we pretended

      to own a new

mattress.   The monster never slept

    through the night—

        she chucked

cell phones against the walls,   mixed kisses

      and drugs, owned sin

        like a steady stream

  of urine on a stick.   Once,

        I named her Perversion.

   Once, I named her   The Accident.

      Once, there was

no name.   I tried to evict

   her,   but outside

      there were too many worlds,

too many centers,   too many

bombs.   Instead, I sang to her about the wind

                                        and the candle, when a car

crushed a princess,   and everything stopped.

            I told her to perform   flesh is to forget

the mess.   Everywhere

            is the basement,   you are the only

    piece   of furniture

                              to survive.

TRAINING

The puppy won't stop eating rocks and moss.
Sometimes I pry open her mouth to find

whole splinters of bark on her pink tongue. We try
to train her to sit, to stick out

her paw when we ask. When she poops in the house,
we bring it to the yard so she knows where to go

next time. And later, after it's dried in the sun, after the flies
have had their fill, we scoop it up and throw it in the woods.

Here, the world is perpetual March,
and we love a dog as if that's the only thing we can do, as if

death cannot touch this slice of New England, the trees
growing a canopy of shade just for us.

Yesterday, we strapped the smallest life jacket
to her furry body, took her swimming for the first time.

We watched her paddle from the shore to the center of the lake,
then back again until she grew tired. And last night

while we argued about things that won't
matter in a month, he was still petting the puppy's wet head,

and I cried like I'd never known a kindness
so pure and gentle as that, as a pat on the head

for doing nothing but existing. I wouldn't
call this jealousy, but I have no word

in my human tongue that seems appropriate.
It's the feeling of all the stones I swallowed in my youth

growing jagged in my belly. And I scratch
the surface of my skin with any sharp thing

I can find to cut them out.

SAD GIRL SONNET #1

Even in the most beautiful city, you can still be
sad as fuck. There is the Duomo, Palazzo Vecchio,
and the waiter from the bar downstairs who shouts *bella!*
as you pass. I've been eating Doritos on the couch again,
I've been blocking out my noise, watching QVC
in Italian, I want to buy useless shit
even more. The way the woman describes the sweater—
lunghi, taglia, nero—I need it. I need someone to say

fall in love, fall for the city, fall on your hands
and knees and suck your fingers for practice. Last month,
was there a hidden grace to peeing with the door
open? He said he liked to watch, and now
no one sees me lift up the seat, hover
over the bowl. Every city has a sewer.

SAD GIRL SONNET #2

Last week I had breakfast with a lover

        from three years ago. I confessed

nothing, the yolk from the over-

        easy egg crusting in the grooves

of my thumb ring. I'd like to believe it's a sign

        for something. They change

the pH, you know. Dicks, not eggs.

        They can't leave anything they enter

quietly. So I'm on Tinder in Italy. I'm on

        Klonopin in Italy, Wellbutrin, gabapentin,

Plan B. Here it's called ellaOne.

        The Italians can make any morning

after sound romantic, church bells

        in the distance, sperm running down my thigh.

SAD GIRL SONNET #4

I made a wish for you on a bridge in Venice
covered in lovers' locks. In this dimension,

I've sucked another dick
to forget yours. In this dimension

the rain falls, and the city drains slurp it
down. It floods every year, and the people

walk on platforms through Piazza San Marco
as if land were a luxury. And it's been a year,

of a lonely needful act, I scroll through
videos of naked women to remember my body.

In another dimension, we're eating western omelets
before we shower together. In another dimension,

the cat paws at the curtain, trying to catch
the water from the wrong side.

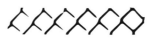

PEOPLE WHO DON'T UNDERSTAND MENTAL ILLNESS

are always full of advice—*look on the bright side,*
do yoga, snap out of it. I'm supposed to put
my feet in the wet grass, touch the sponge
of the earth underneath me—that's what
my beloved suggests after I have wasted myself
on the pain of the unknown. Enough with distractions,
enough watching *Temptation Island* reruns, creating
scenarios where I am the jealous woman watching
her lover take body shots off some busty blonde.
I'm really just sad about death. All the deaths
this season makes and remakes. So I put
my feet in the damn grass, get them as wet
and grassy as I possibly can, stomp them
like a child playing in the mud. If I'm going
to take his advice, I'm going to go all out. If being
cured were as easy as putting my feet in the grass,
fuck, cover me in a spring's worth of clippings.
Aren't I supposed to try to love it again,
the spring? Each spring, another Jesus to resurrect,
each spring another rotten egg. I thought
I was supposed to leave all my bodies
buried. But I look for them, my fingers
deep in the mud now, scraping the ground
with what nail stubs I have left.

AND THEN FINALLY

One afternoon I pretended to run away,
packed my pink hamper with only the essentials—

my Barbies and the Ken doll they shared,
a blanket, a pillow, galletas María, and a Sunny Delight.

I balanced the hamper on top of my toy baby carriage
and wheeled it around the living room, into the kitchen,

hauled it up the stairs, then back down again. I even
brought it into the bathroom and sat on the toilet,

swinging my legs, galaxy underwear dangling like a hammock.
I don't know why the performance of leaving

was a kind of magic, an adventure to nowhere, navigating
the terrain of our small apartment. My mother

didn't ask questions. Instead, she watched
me drag my belongings through each room

as I practiced fate, practiced my birthright
to bruise. I learned that love was like the red rose

after the blue on my mother's arms. Some days
each corner of our apartment smelled of bouquets

in different stages of death, some
still fresh with days before rot, before mold

fuzzed on the base of their stems, or the petals fell
like molted scales. Maybe the day I pretended to leave

smelled like the funeral only neglect can make,
blossoms to mask the decay, blossoms

to shroud the bride. Freedom is
a girl rehearsing despair, and despair

is a woman and a U-Haul leaving Brooklyn.
The truth is I packed too many things,

though I left behind the pilón, the cake tin,
and the condoms. And I knew where I'd end up—

back at my mother's with the flowers, their thorny stems
cut on a bias, placed in a glass vase by the TV, static

mimicking the sound from my mouth.

SEASONAL AFFECTIVE

Spencer-Peirce-Little Farm, 2014

After a freeze
there is a thaw. The once-revered Christmas
trees now litter the sidewalks, their living-room
glory used up, no longer worthy of lights and tinsel, glittered
ornaments. Instead, their branches droop over the edge
like fainting women's arms, pine-needle confetti
from the party you weren't invited to.
I've been so accustomed to the plastic
trees living in the basement
for eleven months, not the luxury
of plucking life to let it fade.

Here, burning
is tradition. Once I went to a farm where the people
sipped hot chocolate while waiting for sundown,
when the local fire department would set
a hill of Christmas trees ablaze—
all the fainting ladies bright again, stars
born from the best trash.

After the burning
was more burning, his hands reached
to unbutton my sweater, then made a canopy
of my arms when he took off my tank top,
discarding it to the corner of the room.
What if I am given only one
season of light? A quick
peak, a pleasure blown out, a little
flame on top of a cake. Candles
are for more than birthdays, also sex,
survival.

After that thaw
was the worst freeze, the puddles all black,
the ash—ambered in ice.

DIARY ENTRY #29: POLARIZATION

I wonder if I will spend the winter
putting on my grandmothered grief.

I'm becoming a church, a funeral,
an aquarium with no men. There is

a mermaid in my dream of the brothers—
I love them both—and the mermaid

shows me the underwater apple trees, the fruit
ripe to be picked. I'm no angel

but I need to voyage the land
between crisis and hope, land

like doom understood. I am
a warrior of not letting go,

and the brothers need to drown.
I could threaten the sea

with my drawer of small things.
I could dangle language like an heirloom,

like bloodied lace on a body without name.
Would the sea take them, beautiful

brothers of before and after. The condoms
still sleep on the streets

where I threw them like petals. O
wedding, O bomb—I dance

on the table like a widow, bread
and butter in my toes.

AFTER MY STEPFATHER LEAVES, MY MOTHER OPENS THE WINDOWS

to let out the smell of Old Spice,
and fish head soup, the leftover
mondongo lingering in the fridge.

> In 2001, he lingers on the bed, slips
> his hand under my shirt.

> In 1994, he buys Niagara Falls T-shirts
> for my sister & me after we ride
> the *Maid of the Mist,* the blue ponchos
> sticking to our wet legs, the sign
> threatens, *Get on board for an electric experience.*

I threaten my mother with running
away if she lets him come back
this time, if his Buick is parked in the driveway.

> In 2007, he teaches me how to parallel park
> in the lot at Chunky's Cinema,
> which will close in 2019
> when I forget how to parallel park.

> In 2021, I forget what year
> I first saw bruises on her arms.

My mother bruises the kitchen tile with the slap
of the wet mop. She points the fan
downward so the floor dries before the dog
muddies it with her paws. We listen to the rush.

In 1992, she listens to the radio preacher and
calls in a prayer request—she asks God
to protect her family.

In 1997, her family watches her place
a ring on the preacher's finger. I scatter
flower petals down the aisle.

I scatter fish heads in the yard.

In 1997, on my brother's head
the preacher leaves a welt.

ICONIC MAKEOVER SCENE

All the TikTok tutorials say only the ring
finger is allowed there, only a gentle tap of serum

before bed. I'm not supposed to crash
my hand into my face, fingers kissing me crimson. I bruise

my eye because I can't bruise another's. I thought the fall
would do me a favor. September comes and I still

want. There are no precious seasons left, just
the couch and reruns of *Roswell,* leftover lo mein

and chicken wings barely naked, neglected
meat dangling off the bone. My beloved

saw me become the father. And I was
good at it. I matched myself to the colors

of the turning maple in the yard—
yellow and brown, from margin to tip

an ombré of red.

DIARY ENTRY #33: LOVE SONG

I haven't stopped stealing chapsticks from Target. I haven't
stopped questioning the afterlife. My mother
sings to me every year and I'm still
dying. I'm measuring distances
by the ache in my throat, the border
of my body, navel to pussy. Is this
my punishment for slipping the small cylinders
so easily into my pocket? I have faith
that all the pretty people
are prettier than me and all the pretty people
are geographically out of reach.
Even though I've left
a seat for Elijah, I don't deserve
forgiveness for the hunger. Tell me, what is the shape
of your starved bloat? Is it shaped
like the bartender from Tuesday night, or
the Brooklyn Bridge? Could mine
be shaped like the Cabbage Patch doll
that I fed a glass of water, the rate
at which the stuffed face grew. I want
to believe he didn't damage me
like a dirty little whore, like leaving
a syndrome for a band-aid. Sometimes
touching is the only food around. Sometimes
I set a table for the wounds.

MY THERAPIST CALLS THESE PATTERNS

I call them an inheritance, my mother
      and the mothers before. I am a mother
            to something. I conceived a child

with what fear owed me—a wet finger in my mouth,
      a hand between my thighs. When I opened
            my cracked earth, I upset the frozen

lake like the time we drove on Winnipesaukee
      to watch the ice fishers drill holes.
            The car got stuck for two hours. Isn't it all

a retelling? Another New England town, another
      season to be left on the twin
            bed with the flowered quilt.

After the pills, there is always a bright
      room, a distorted My Little Pony scene, a static
            rising from the rainbow in the distance. Destruction

loves me, clogs the showers, leaves me
      scooping cups of water and pouring them
            into the toilet. I keep freezing

lovers in the lake. Mostly, I am
      the villain in the room. I forget to stop
            for the possum crossing the road, babies

on her back. Death is never
      deserved, but it comes anyway. The double
            yellow line spattered with blood, the three

smaller copies crowning her head.

IN PORTLAND, IT RAINS, THE SUN COMES OUT, IT HAILS, THE SUN COMES OUT

then it rains again. The ants find their way
to the kitchen counter where I spilled a little sugar,
the spider by the nightstand is the second-to-last
lover I'd want to wake up next to. The doctor says
I have an abscess on my tonsil and for three days
I can't swallow my spit without wincing. The wind
makes the house creak, which sounds
like someone trying to break into my sick nest.
At night from the window, I see six deer
eating from the bushes, and I am glad to witness
this all-you-can-eat buffet. WebMD says
I could die, but I already knew that.
My beloved and I argue through a screen,
and it's the first time I hear how pathetic
this voice can be. Then I smash the spider
with my shoe. And the hail starts again.
In the morning, the dead spider vibrates
under the swarm of ants covering it, eating.

ANOTHER POEM ABOUT NATURE, BUT REALLY IT'S ABOUT ME

I'm not used to all this nature—the robin and the blue

jay perch on the railing outside my window while I sip coffee,

the centipede scurries in the sink next to the dirty spoon. I leave

the birds alone but the centipede has to go. I name it

Ben after one of my exes and drown it, send it

down the drain. All exes live there, down

the drain where they've crawled out of the pipe

sludge to the clean stainless steel of the undermount

sink. By the way, this is a borrowed kitchen. By the way,

this is a borrowed life. I don't belong in a log cabin

in the woods where the squirrels are actually startled. I want

the don't-give-a-fuck attitude of a New York squirrel,

eating from the palms of whoever has something to give—

the leftover crumbs from the morning's bacon-egg-and-cheese

or the last bit of falafel dipped in hummus from Mamoun's.

But wasn't that a borrowed life too? I was supposed to be

a preacher's wife, skirt to my ankles, Bible

in my purse. And I was supposed to be a mother. The doctors

don't know if this body can cradle the egg

before it's flushed. And I'm not supposed to be jealous

of the birds, or the squirrel, or the drowned centipede,

how easy it was to blame it, let the water run.

SAD GIRL SONNET #9

I'm an inspiration for returning—
the married man goes back to his wife, puts his lips
back on the beer bottle. I return to a country
that loved me once, get drunk at the same bars.
In the dressing room, nothing is the right size.
I buy the shirt anyway, save the receipt.
In the Bible, seven years is a short time to grieve,
to work for the same woman. God, I've replaced every Leah
with more Leahs. They're on the screens.
And they're moaning. If I could turn my back on them,
I would. But they're so beautiful and their assholes
are always bleached. I rewind to the part
when the man enters the room. I rewind
to the part when the man enters the room.

SAD GIRL SONNET #10

I've only been away for a month,
and already three men, two pills, two
countries to watch me swallow. I let myself

sing a sad song in the shower today—Toni Braxton's
"Un-Break My Heart," soap trailing down my legs. I shave
my armpits while I cry, feeling for the bumps, a kindness

to my most neglected. No one loves
an ingrown. When I was eleven, my mother hid the razors, hid
me from the men outside, forgetting the one who shared her bed. I press

the blade down to remind myself I could
be alive, if I try hard enough. My mother says
ma' pa'lante hay gente—yes, there are more people ahead

to do damage. What is it to be *un-broken*? I un-cry,
I un-sex, I un-become this.

SAD GIRL SONNET #15

I leave museums too fast, like the men in the morning—
no coffee, maybe a kiss on the cheek, sometimes *I'll call you.*
I stroll by Michelangelo paintings, some da Vinci, whole rooms
of Botticelli. Still, there is no limit to my dissatisfaction
with the world. Nothing feels right, throat burning. I want to go

home. I text the man I've been fucking. I want to love him
but he probably won't let me. I leave Italy in a month.
Sugar has lost all taste, pasta is so yesterday.
But when he kissed me at the very door of Santa Croce,
a bit of the Holy Ghost passed through me, escaped
onto my tongue. And he swallowed it. It's gone. My possessed and tormented

soul. Or maybe it's still here, in my pocket. The phone buzzes,
so I pretend it's you. You're on your way home from work and you ask:
Should I pick up a chicken from Whole Foods?

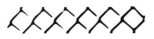

I'M ALMOST 30

and give a good blow job but can't
open a bottle of wine without breaking
the cork. I'm almost 30 and
in my nightmare all of my exes
are meeting for coffee, an unlikely family
of missed orgasms, and I want to say
I'm almost 30 and 30 other women
and I wait in line to pee at a Backstreet Boys concert.
And afterward we all want the same thing, we all want
to fuck a Backstreet Boy tonight. Dear
god, I'm almost 30 and I'm lost
in a funny thing, like looking so beautiful
while the light of the streetlamp falls
perfectly on my skin, and I've survived, or how
my mother's friend who visited me in the hospital each time
is dying of cancer while I run in the street,
my lover chasing me barefoot because
I'm drunk again. So he takes the keys, so he pulls me
inside, and I pretend to sleep on the couch, sneak
out when I hear him snoring, drive
down Main Street with Klonopin
and gin in my belly, and my eyes
are almost 30, blurry with unexpected
sanity like when the guest at the restaurant
touched my arm as she left, handing me the bill, saying
I can't believe you're almost 30 and
with a green speck of nori still stuck in her teeth
she smiled, told me I was a good
waitress, that my energy was warm, and I cried
as I bused the table, because I'm almost 30
and I have so much sin left to live, and more weeks
to leave bloodstains on a mattress, when really

I just want to roll up to every funeral like I own it,
sexy to meet Jesus in a white dress, the runs in my nylons
all fixed with nail polish, and I'm almost 30
and the people in this town
like to watch the piping plovers on the beach,
their orange feet skittering across the shoreline,
like a joy I don't understand, as if
the vastness of the Atlantic wasn't the backdrop,
as if the water couldn't claim
a tiny body for itself,
swallow it whole.

DIARY ENTRY #28: ARS POETICA

I start where I am most afraid: an addiction to beauty
is a place to keep a loss. My father liked to sing love songs, his lips
elongating each vowel, his tongue breaking the center
of everything, and he—so tender to the sound it birthed.
I'm listening to jazz in the park again, crying
in rooms that don't belong to me. It's true—
the wrong music can be damaging and every photograph
is an elegy. I practice posing in bathroom stalls to feel
effortless. All flowers want to be looked at and chasing the moon
is a chronic condition. How can I translate where my finger
lands into language? In conversation, I drop a little French
like a baby out the window. On TV, anyone can be dead
and look like art. A long life is avant-garde—I place mine
on the open shelf, on the edge.

DIARY ENTRY #3: STUDY ON THE NEGATIVE

I want to be the prettiest bird on the internet,
so I pretend they can see me through the motel mirror.
I practice lust, little loon on a bed of no love. The mirror says
my life is not worth the imitation of life. I am
not the favorite, I am not Noah. I am the dumpster
where I find the angel of the Lord spelling my name with nothing
but fortune cookie crumbs, which is not to say
there is hope. No one will believe
it might be a disease making me beautiful
for a limited time. For a limited time, I don't have a will
or testament, but I have this never-ending
emptiness to give away like jewels. Don't
make me out to have value when all I can't do
is exist. I don't need to be a car flipped over on the side
of the road. I've romanticized displaying my mortality
like a da Vinci behind a red velvet rope—
the *Mona Lisa,* slightly awkward, the crowd taking pictures.

I AM THE PATRON SAINT

of leftovers. In my name, the spaghetti
grows a gel of starch, the pesto crusts a ring

around the jar. In my name, I microwave
to the temperature forbidden

to reach. Lukewarm, God spews
me from his mouth, and I weep

like Jesus in the Garden of Gethsemane,
and I kneel on the kitchen floor

mourning the death, but it's just
my own. I collect my relics, my men.

I collect them in a mother's
drawer. I stain the cups

with lipstick, the pubic hair I shave
clogs the drain. To truly disappear,

I take up all the space. I divide
what's left to multiply

a need. It's called mitosis,
it's called ripping

the center. It's called being
made whole.

DIARY ENTRY #10: I WAS NEARLY PERFECT ONCE

before I killed the person I couldn't love. I still see her
shadow. I still use her toilet to vomit what's left
of the latest Taco Bell binge. You know the world
doesn't stop if you undress. If you undress,
all the white boys will still smell the same
when they unshelter you. So I place my cleanliness next
to my evil, so I create a disorder of repetition and protruding
ribs. Without our help, the brain knows what to do—
the migrating birds become black pepper to the sky and the bruised
thigh becomes just another accident. This year
I light a candle on Sylvia's birthday, pretend
to eat the cake, my appetite for a knife on my wrist only a tease
until it's not. Until it's not cake but the earth
and the body I shove into it.

ARE YOU THERE GOD? IT'S ME, YOUR MOTHER

A mother is one of three parts of speech—1. *mother, noun, a female parent,* as in *My mother,*
your mother live across the street 18, 19 Marble Street and every night my mother
is in a fight with my stepfather's fists. 2. *mother, verb, to care for or protect like a mother,*
which is to say, I'm supposed to forgive my mother for not mothering,
for not telling us to climb the tree like the mother
bear in the wildlife documentary, the male sniffing for the mother's
cubs to kill to make her into another mother, and the mother
stands her ground, bares her teeth like the mother of all teeth. 3. *mother,*
adjective, bearing the relation of a mother, which means could I make myself a mother
to anything? I learned from my mother how to be a mother
to my boyfriend, not unlike the children's book I'd heard my mother
read where the bird asks every unmotherly living thing the question, *Are you my mother?*
He didn't know what a mother bird looked like, little mother-
sick bird, seeing mother in the mountain, in the mirror. 4. Another noun, as in *the mother.*

Even vinegar has a mother.

DIARY ENTRY #31: ATTACHMENT DISORDER

Maybe I'm not a mystery: I look
for the father in everyone. *Come home
and hold me,* I say to the exterminator
of all life. I point to the earth
where I'm told duende lives. I point
to the fog my shame has designed.
It is thick and joyless, a soup of ghosts. I've been sad
for too long. For too long, I've been
the kid who needed someone else
to buy her a meal at Bickford's. I order
too much and apologize like I'm dragging a big truth
from under the cement slab in the yard,
my little dog finding the gopher hiding in the dark,
then whipping it in the air by the neck. *Spin,
girl, spin,* they say, the men who don't love me.
And the truth? I believe in hell, not heaven,
because I only know how to perform
a burden. To cling is to build
an altar of collected things: this broken
crayon, that dull knife, another stained shirt.

THE PARABLE

This is how I cry in a new lover's bathroom:
I wipe the cum from my body

that didn't come. I talk to her
like a mother would—O little

clit, little clit, so many
have neglected you, so many

have licked and lost.
Little clit, little clit, why do love

and dying feel the same?
It's a sad life for us

of dipping fries in barbecue sauce
while sitting in our own mother's living room.

I'm always mourning something—
the yellow dress I wore, the first kiss

outside the Tenement Museum, the chemistry
of spit. *Bodies aren't reliable witnesses,*

the midwife on TV says to a woman
with a phantom in her womb.

What is *reliable*? The body can't keep
a promise, not like God can

when I asked Him to make me
sick if I ever left Him so I would know

I had strayed, asked Him to break
my bony leg like a shepherd to his lost

sheep. And I'm sick, so sick, little
clit. Little clit, do you hear me?

We have to go back.

FISHING OUT THE CONDOM HAS ME BELIEVING IN GOD

again. I reach in with my index finger, get swallowed
by the grooved flesh. I escape a baby like Jonah
escaped Nineveh. Is this what it means to be loved
by the Lord, swallowed by His whale? The man
from the internet says he'll pay for the pill and fast
forward, he doesn't. Tomorrow I will drive to three
pharmacies just to unbaby me. Maybe this
was God's will after all—I am thrown
overboard by the loss of my beloved. I build
a throne for mourning—McChicken
wrappers and cans of ginger ale. When the beloved
yelled, sometimes it was my fault, sometimes
I knew better than to leave my little need out
where he could see. I pry open the plastic
with kitchen scissors and place the singular, scored
pill in my palm. After three days, my body will bleed
out my prophet as if nothing ever happened.

MONSTER IS GOOD AT BREAKUPS

I say this to the mirror in the bar bathroom, gin
and tonic and lime still tacky on my fingers. I've
downloaded the app. I've downloaded
need. Instagram therapists have confirmed: I'm addicted
to reassurance. Who wouldn't be addicted to feeling?
I'm supposed to learn how to hurt and not lean
into ideation. I lean up against the sink,
check my teeth. I think about expanding
my radius. More area means more chances means more
people to love or fuck or fail. I'm better at the last two.
Monster is not good at goodbyes. Monster is not
good. Monster wants steak dinner. Monster wants new
lipstick and new lips to kiss. Monster wants
a baby. Monster wants to kill me.

SAD GIRL SONNET #18

The summer I moved to New York was the summer of BV:
bacterial vaginosis. I wanted to blame the subway platform
heat. Or the new silk underwear I bought to feel like Carrie Bradshaw,
my true *Sex and the City* moment, and here was BV, stinky
BV, me and BV at my fourth visit to the health center already.
I want to blame a dick. But I don't know whose
to blame. I could blame my pussy, her distorted rainbow
of brown, deeper brown, pink, red, and purple. She's so
innocent. At lunch, the Italian molds a pussy out of ham,
prosciutto cotto drizzled in oil, sprinkled with salt and ground
pepper. Ham pussy is on a fresh slice of bread, ham
pussy doesn't move when he places
her in his mouth, when he bites. She's so quiet
and respectful. I'm almost jealous.

SAD GIRL SONNET #19

It's another Tuesday, and I marvel at what I can—the interwoven
    curves of a pretzel-shaped cookie covered in sugar crystals,
just one variety in the blue tin. My grandmother
    was a beautiful woman—I think this while I sip my coffee
alone in a foreign country, remembering how she used
    the empty tins for sewing kits. Why does everything feel
like dying? I chew this cookie now, but I will die. The last time,
    I stopped myself because I was afraid of a hell. I've been told
there is the most beautiful fresco of hell in Pisa. I need to know
    my options. One of the cookies in the tin
looks like a rippled teardrop, hole in the center, and for an hour
    I'm mad at the person who designed the hole there. I dip
the cookie, and the coffee flows right in. To be
    passed through with ease. How could hell be worse.

SAD GIRL SONNET #25

On Via Calimala, I window-shop and look at things
I can never own—Gucci, Guess, and Miss Sixty. I watch the couples

holding hands as they walk out of each store. They are ads
for a promised life. I want that purse. I want those heels,

I want that ring on her finger. I mourn
to prepare for more mourning. I can't get the painted Madonnas

out of my head—her blue shawl, and baby Jesus with his hand
down her shirt, or on her cheek, two little fingers

raised to the sky. It's a sign of the coming, his cleaving to her breast,
a fate understood. God, I want to understand my fate—

who will fuck me and stay. I cleave to their shirts
when I kiss them at the door. I search the windows, the alleys,

the internet, for the fingers that will touch me something
prophetic. All I ask is for a death or resurrection.

DIARY ENTRY #34: EPIGENETICS

It's been eight years
and the ancestors in me are still
burdened. I don't know if I am gentle with them.
I reheat the coffee in the microwave,
find gratitude when they take what's theirs
and leave the rest. There will always be
scarcity—less food, less Klonopin—
which is to say I own a legacy of fear.
Tonight, another grandmother is dying,
and I cannot heal her. But I line up
my idols like bruises on my belly
and perform a nostalgic ritual:
I shower with my clothes on
like I did as a girl with a man
who wanted to be my father,
when I became a little bird, helpless
to affection. Did he make me
a good monster or a bad one?
I can keep my cage clean,
wipe my mouth with my thumb.

ANOTHER POEM ABOUT GOD, BUT REALLY IT'S ABOUT ME

You would've made a lousy nun, the woman
on the A train says to the person on the other end

of the phone. I laugh to no one and imagine
what a lousy nun would do—maybe sneak

a lover into her room on Ash Wednesday or take
off her wedding ring from God, let the sun

touch the unveiled skin. I was never
a nun, but I was called *Sister,* and Brothers

were not allowed to do more than shake
my hand. I was called *daughter* when the pastor

kissed my cheek, when I was worth more than rubies.
I was a good Sister for a decade—I was

good. After I left, I still prayed to all the Fathers
who weren't mine. I opened my mouth

to their wisdom, and in my tongue was the law
of kindness. I became their Mary

Magdalene—holy by day, whore by night—
perfuming the feet of every man named

Jesus. After I left, I stayed devout—
devout to recklessness, devout to taking

out my virgin. I don't remember craving
anything so much as my own destruction.

It was beautiful to watch from the bleachers
of my mind, separating myself from

all the Sisters inside me. In Proverbs,
it is virtuous for a woman to work willingly

with her hands. I only wanted to bring virtue
unto my name when I held each new body in my palms.

I only wanted to bring virtue when I hid
in the bathroom, slapped my face.

DIARY ENTRY #6: SESTINA

I remember staining my life at the cross
like any good church girl, my sin
crushed like a dead bird, ground
under God's finger, laid next to the sin of the girls
before me. I murdered my only dove for Him,
when I offered her mid-preen, her back

turned to His light. I could not turn back
to my old life—I had crossed
another Jordan—I broke my phone, broke my moon for him.
It was impossible to be the best, the sin
taking over like the mold in the bathroom, the girls
popping the heads of the mushrooms growing from the walls, not the ground.

Sometimes I pretended to be immoral, my hands on the ground,
not in the air to praise. I used to pour out my spirit back
then, not a Joan of Arc but just another girl
in love. I sang songs about strawberry wine and crossed
my fingers, hoping the *hot July moon* wouldn't see my sin
explode like stars against the car windshield, my legs wrapped around him.

But the guilt kept its promise, my good Good Samaritan. I'd fail Him
again, I knew. I was my own maker of disposal, the ground
still wet with my passion. What is a boy, but a supermagnet for sin?
To quote The Book felt X-rated—my virginity growing back
only to be thirsted for by the boys. So I threw up the cross
on the cross, I threw up the bird, I threw up the girl,

I threw up the scrambled eggs from breakfast—is this what it meant to be a girl
lost to the world? I was infested with regret, I crumbled to Him
and him. On purpose, I forgot to look both ways when I crossed

the street, traffic meeting me as gentle as a tickle on my toes, the ground
a feather on my face. So I tried mixing butter and suicide. Back
then, I blossomed sadder than a nunnery. Sin

was sewn into me, grew with me, my sin
supersized. Smaller and smaller the girl
in me became, leaving the little whore so strong now, her back
hairy like a beard, my beautiful whore. I tried to forget about Him.
I took my whore to college, she kissed the ground
outside the library with her painted lips. She uncrossed

her legs and I loved her back. I wrapped her warm in the sin
of every finger I crossed inside her. And I fed her pizza. No girl
would need Him, so we broke Him, buried Him in the ground.

MY EX MEETS FOR COFFEE

When he leaves the café, my panties
are still dry. He can't conjure
me anymore. Instead, I wet myself
with thoughts of licking
my finger in the bathroom,
of pleasure without his name. I want
to say my own name, chant it.
Are you there me? It's
me. Which is to say I am the hand
that slapped my face in the middle of the street
that night in June, then that other night
in June. I fell to the pavement and someone
caught my arm. Maybe I am perpetually
bored—that is a disease of the mind.
I want to be the ruined woman who stays
alive. Anna Karenina jumped in front of a train,
Madame Bovary with arsenic, and me
with the same pills as last time. I want to have
an affair and not feel guilty, escape
the provincial life I'll never live.
I might be a glutton for gluttony. I've been
promised a fatness, one with an inventory
of things to count—dresses and curtains
and microwave ovens, La Croix
to drown in, a pillowtop bed. I make
a Pinterest board of the good life,
touch myself to the teal green of my imagined

KitchenAid mixer. In my mind, I'm rolling
in sheets of Egyptian cotton, and I feel
a blessing from inside me release.

BLESSING THE BABY

When my upstairs neighbor invites me to her baby shower,

      I feel guilty about forgetting to bring in my recycling bins,

again. I am a bad neighbor, but she's going to be a mother

      so she'll have to practice forgiveness on someone first. Usually,

I'm a people pleaser. I am a people. I was born

      with all of the people I could ever create inside me. I try

to forgive them—their dirty handprints on my skirt, their towels

      left on the bathroom floor. We blessed the baby

while we tied around our wrists one long, red string.

      For a moment, the string connected us—wives, mothers,

and me, neither—until it didn't, until the scissors severed

      us, made a bracelet of the blood string. I told the baby,

I give you this wrist. The world will break all your blessings

      if it wants, and believe me, baby, most of the time, it wants.

WANTING

I want to write about joy—I decide this when I sit down at my desk,
the overwatered succulents lining the perimeter. I don't

understand the ratio of plant to water to dirt, so I drown
them in what I think is needed. I forget sun.

I forget patience. I try to forget the look death makes—
the *Haworthia,* the snake plant, my grandmother, the dog.

I wanted to write about joy. Everything is pale.
Outside, winter persists, even though it's May.

A lover once told me he believed in the risk
of joy, used it to explain away the kiss on my neck.

He's married now, *the risk of joy* tattooed on the right side
of his own neck, his new wife's name on the left.

My friend said I dodged a bullet with that one, I say
I would've opened my chest to it.

ANOTHER POEM ABOUT AN EX, BUT REALLY IT'S ABOUT ME

At the grocery store, he gives each avocado

a gentle squeeze before putting it in the basket.

For a moment, I marvel at this quotidian

tenderness, then write it down

so I can put it here in this poem. We go back

to his studio apartment in Brooklyn,

a converted storefront, where he cuts

open an avocado for lunch, scrapes the inner

skin clean, offering me the buttery meat

on a spoon. He sucks the pit, wasting

nothing as he smashes what's left on toast. We have

sex after that, in the heat of June with no AC,

his cat still sleeping at the foot of the bed. It's been

years, and I still haven't forgotten the avocados

in his hands, the fingernails chewed down, yellowed

with nicotine, the skin jagged. Back then,

I didn't want any other hand but that one—

that hand on the small of my back leading me

through Broadway, that hand on my knee

while riding the train as it screeched forward

into the dark. And now there is another

hand I'm learning to love, soft fingers and calloused

palms, careful as he cracks each egg into the pan.

The part of the poem that's about me is this:

the poem is already about me, this keen eye

ready to find another moment to make

the heart swell. I find something to love

like I find air in a room. I just walk in.

I HAVEN'T BEEN ON A PLANE SINCE THE WORLD ENDED

That's the sentence I overhear at Logan Airport,
where just a few moments ago my beloved kissed me
for what will be the last time
for a month. *I miss you already,* he texts
not long after dropping me off at Terminal A
and driving back home to New Hampshire, a state
I didn't imagine living in, just another brown girl
in a crowd of white people—I might add here, reader,
my beloved is white and when I hold his hand in public
it feels like the gentlest *fuck you.* When the world ended
and came back, I decided to stay
this time. I've decided to stay many times,
but I'm surprised when I actually go through
with the staying, as much as I am surprised
when the woman next to me in the security check line
comforts her restless baby sitting in the covered carriage
and instead of a cry, a pathetic meow rises
from underneath the blanket. There is no
baby just a cat, which at first feels like a metaphor for my life,
but I'm not even a mother to a cat. I am a mother
to this hunger. I am waiting for the smallest bag
of cheese crackers to fill the unfillable
hole. When I have waited my turn and heard
the adequate number of snaps and pops
from opened cans, enough of the crinkle
of plastic wrappers, the flight attendant hands out
the tiny snacks, and I'm supposed to feel blessed
as the little rhinestones on each of her manicured nails
sends a whisper of light to my broken soul.
Then the layover in Salt Lake City leaves me
crying in a bathroom stall for an hour
because I can, because I have five hours to kill. The truth is

I'm not used to feeling good or even
just okay, and I'm frightened I'll turn healthy
and boring. I'm going away to write in the woods,
and I'm still waiting for the nervous
breakdown to catch me. I'm too prepared this time—
I've stocked up on all the metaphorical
toilet paper and hand sanitizer I can find. I've stolen
all the baby wipes from the babies. There is nothing
left to do but wait.

WE NEVER STOP TALKING ABOUT OUR MOTHERS

Renee and I, hers—in the urn by her desk,
and mine—alive in an apartment forty minutes
from here, probably watching a telenovela, frying
plantains, texting me good night. Renee's mother isn't
really in the urn. She's in the blue wall,
the beach landscape painting, the dog
barking at the unexpected, the jangle of silver bracelets.
We are all carrying our mothers, and we are all better
daughters with the dead. She tells me I am wise,
and all I can think about are the moments of my unwiseness: driving
and sipping margaritas from a water bottle, the bruise
on my arm and taking him back. Her husband
is away at the family cabin, and she is glad
for the space. My husband doesn't exist, and I am
sad for the space I make my home in. I buy sunflowers
and goat cheese, throw a dinner party for the ghosts.
I don't know Renee's mother's name to send a proper invitation.
I don't know the names of the women in my family
past my great-grandmother. How will I call upon them
when it's time? Will I call them *Mary* or *Venus*
or *Yemaya*? I've yet to burn the palo santo, the sage.
I want to leave behind a legacy of light.
I want to leave someone better.

AFTER THE FIRST NIGHT ALONE, SOMEWHERE NEW

I'm up too early organizing my pills
in the drawer I'll only use for a month,
and the shampoo in the shower—always label facing out.
Home is where my compulsions are, home is where
I've cried the most. In Brooklyn
every L train was home, those late nights
or early mornings of giving in
to what I thought I deserved. I deserved
less than love then. I deserved the shriek
of the subway, digging the city
from underneath my fingernails. Home
was where the water turned grey, washing
my hands caked with New York's daily
gift. Once, I was taught that home was where
God's people were, and I believed it,
wagged my tongue in a language
I don't speak anymore. In this language,
I love you could have sounded like a trippy
Sound of Music, like shuffling the solfège syllables—
si do re mi fa la fa la sol ti re mi—over and
over until the trance left you falling out,
the Spirit waiting to catch you. I would've fallen
for any lord. I would've fallen for the fallen
angel himself, if he promised me
belonging, the intoxicating smell
of my beloved's shirt, the armpits
ripe with it.

ANNIVERSARY

Outside, an abandoned mattress sags with rain
and the driveway turns all sludge when I remember
I could've died eight years ago, in a bed
smaller than the one I share with a new lover
who just this morning found another grey hair in my afro,
and before resettling the wiry curl with the others,
kissed the freckle on my forehead.
I admit, I don't know a love that doesn't
destroy. Last night while we slept,
a mouse drowned in the rice pot
I left soaking in the sink. I tried
to make a metaphor out of this, the way
he took the mouse to the edge of the lake in the yard,
released it to a deeper grave. It was
an anniversary: just my lover
taking a dead thing away, taking it
somewhere I couldn't see.

I BUY MY MONSTER ROSES

Though the people on the internet help too.
They send money by pressing a small button
on their screens. It would be disingenuous
to claim all the credit—we can't heal

or hurt alone. I sniff the top of each rose
like a newborn's scalp—fresh skin and hair
only a few days picked. I try to arrange the flowers
on my bed, create a romantic scene

like all the '90s rom-coms I still watch. I'm stuck
in the past, I know. I'm stuck in the present,
I know that too. I thought the roses
could be a cure, and maybe in a small way

they were, each petal I plucked so gently
from the stems gave in to me.

NOTES

All "Diary Entry" poems are collages written with lines collected from thirty-six-and-counting personal journals I've kept since age nine. The number in the title corresponds to the number of the journal used in the creation of that poem.

"Someday I'll Stop Killing Diannely Antigua" was written after Frank O'Hara's "Katy."

"Self-Portrait as Easter Pamphlet on the Door" was written borrowing words from the Jehovah's Witness magazine *The Watchtower.*

"After My Stepfather Leaves, My Mother Opens the Windows" was written after Jane Wong's "After My Father Leaves, My Mother Opens the Windows."

"Sad Girl Sonnet #9" references the biblical story of Jacob and two of his wives, Leah and Rachel, both daughters of Laban. Jacob first fell in love with Rachel and worked for her father, Laban, for seven years in order to make her his bride. After the seven years, Laban tricked him and gave him Leah to marry instead. Jacob was allowed to marry Rachel in return for seven more years of labor.

"Are You There God? It's Me, Your Mother" is a play on the title of Judy Blume's novel *Are You There God? It's Me, Margaret.* "My Ex Meets for Coffee" includes a line that plays on this title as well.

"The Parable" borrows a line from the show *Call the Midwife* (season 8, episode 5).

"Fishing Out the Condom Has Me Believing in God" is after Taneum Bambrick's poem "This breakup has me believing in god."

"Diary Entry #6: Sestina" borrows a line from the song "Strawberry Wine" by Deana Carter.

"Wanting" was written after Marie Howe's poem "Wanting a Child."

"After the First Night Alone, Somewhere New" references the song "Do-Re-Mi" sung by Julie Andrews in *The Sound of Music*.

"I Buy My Monster Roses" would have not been possible without the generous folks from the internet who gifted me the funds to buy the most beautiful bouquet of flowers, many of them roses, to honor my grandmother Rosa Aybar on the 10th anniversary of her passing.

Listen to the *Good Monster* playlist on Spotify. A song accompanies each poem. https://bit.ly/goodmonsterbydiannelyantigua

ACKNOWLEDGMENTS

Thank you to the following literary journals and anthologies that published many of the poems in this book, sometimes in earlier versions or with different titles:

Academy of American Poets Poem-a-Day: "Anniversary" and "Blessing the Baby"

The Adroit Journal: "Sad Girl Sonnet #2" and "Sad Girl Sonnet #19"

Alchemy: "I Haven't Been on a Plane since the World Ended"

Apogee: "People Who Don't Understand Mental Illness"

Black Warrior Review: "In Portland, It Rains, the Sun Comes Out, It Hails, the Sun Comes Out"

BOAAT Journal: "And Then Finally"

Brink: "Diary Entry #10: I Was Nearly Perfect Once" and "My Ex Meets for Coffee"

Cherry Tree: "My Therapist Calls These Patterns" and "Sad Girl Sonnet #25"

Copper Nickel: "Diary Entry #3: Study on the Negative"

Couplet Poetry: "Sad Girl Sonnet #15" and "Sad Girl Sonnet #18"

Cordella Magazine: "Self-Portrait as Easter Pamphlet on the Door" and "Connections"

Daughters of Latin America Anthology: An International Anthology of Writing by Latine Women: "Sad Girl Sonnet #10"

Indiana Review: "Fishing Out the Condom Has Me Believing in God"

Narrative: "We Never Stop Talking about Our Mothers"

Northwest Review: "Diary Entry #34: Epigenetics"

Pangyrus: "Chronically"

Pigeon Pages: "Diary Entry #12: The Monster" and "Seasonal Affective"

Poetry: "Training," "Diary Entry #28: Ars Poetica," and "Diary Entry #31: Attachment Disorder"

Poetry Northwest: "Wanting"

Pouch: "I Am the Patron Saint"

Prairie Schooner: "After the First Night Alone, Somewhere New"

Redivider: "Someday I'll Stop Killing Diannely Antigua"

Rough Cut Press: "Pantoum in Case of Emergency"

Split Lip Magazine: "I'm Almost 30"

The Massachusetts Review: "Diary Entry #5: Self-Portrait as Revelations" and "A Hundred and Then None"

The Cortland Review: "Diary Entry #13: Being Sick Is a Romantic Idea" and "Diary Entry #29: Polarization"

Trnsfr: "Diary Entry #33: Love Song"

Tupelo Quarterly: "Diary Entry #6: Sestina"

Vox Viola: "I'm Surprised at My Tolerance," "Sad Girl Sonnet #1," "Sad Girl Sonnet #4," "Sad Girl Sonnet #9," and "The Parable"

Waxwing: "Another Poem about God, but Really It's about Me," "Another Poem about Nature, but Really It's about Me," and "I Buy My Monster Roses"

A monstrous amount of thanks to the editors and staff at Copper Canyon Press for taking what was once just a Word document and making it into the book you're now holding in your hands. A special thanks to Michael and Ash, for reading and rereading every sad poem with such care.

Thank you to my family for their support since the beginning, when I was just a child scribbling on little pieces of paper. As my mother always says, I love you to the moon and back.

Thank you to the community that has fostered my growth as a writer, as it takes a village to raise one: Haverhill Public Library, Northern Essex Community College, UMass Lowell, the UMass Lowell Centers for Learning, the UMass Boston Creative Writing MFA Program, the NYU Creative Writing Program, NYU Florence, Universidad de Sevilla, CantoMundo, Community of Writers, the Fine Arts Work Center, the Academy of American Poets, Brooklyn Poets, HAVEN, Word Market, NH PANTHER, University of New Hampshire, the Nossrat Yassini Poetry Festival, the Whiting Foundation, the Mellon Foundation, YesYes Books, Carolyn Moore Writing Residency, Book & Bar, The Press Room, The Wilder, and the Portsmouth Poet Laureate Program.

Another monstrous amount of thanks to my press sibling, Kayleb Rae Candrilli, for handling this manuscript with all the tenderness as they helped me organize the pages for the first time on the floor of the Carolyn Moore Writers House.

Thank you to the endless snacks that fueled me while editing this book. I'm indebted to your salt and sugar.

Thank you to my loves, my friends, my succulents, my little apartment.

Thank you to Cindy for being my merchant of hope.

Thank you to my monster. I wrote this for you, little one.

ABOUT THE AUTHOR

Diannely Antigua is a Dominican American poet and educator, born and raised in Massachusetts. Her debut collection *Ugly Music* (YesYes Books, 2019) was the winner of the Pamet River Prize and a 2020 Whiting Award. She received her BA in English from the University of Massachusetts Lowell, where she won the Jack Kerouac Creative Writing Scholarship, and received her MFA at NYU, where she was awarded a Global Research Initiative Fellowship to Florence, Italy. She is the recipient of additional fellowships from CantoMundo, Community of Writers, and the Fine Arts Work Center Summer Program, and was a finalist for the 2021 Ruth Lilly and Dorothy Sargent Rosenberg Poetry Fellowship. Her work has been nominated for the Pushcart Prize and chosen for *The Best of the Net Anthology*. Her poems can be found in Poem-a-Day, *Poetry, The American Poetry Review, Washington Square Review, The Adroit Journal,* and elsewhere. She currently teaches in the MFA Program in Writing at the University of New Hampshire as the inaugural Nossrat Yassini Poet in Residence. She is the host of the podcast *Bread & Poetry* and resides in Portsmouth, New Hampshire, where she is the poet laureate, the youngest person, and the first person of color, to receive that title.

Poetry is vital to language and living. Since 1972, Copper Canyon Press has published extraordinary poetry from around the world to engage the imaginations and intellects of readers, writers, booksellers, librarians, teachers, students, and donors.

WE ARE GRATEFUL FOR THE MAJOR SUPPORT PROVIDED BY:

academy of american poets

OFFICE OF ARTS & CULTURE
SEATTLE

amazon literary partnership

THE PAUL G. ALLEN
FAMILY FOUNDATION

4
CULTURE

Hawthornden Foundation

INGRAM
CONTENT GROUP

the point
envision·enact·evolve

Lannan

WASHINGTON STATE
ARTS COMMISSION

ART WORKS. National Endowment for the Arts arts.gov

The Witter Bynner Foundation
for Poetry

TO LEARN MORE ABOUT UNDERWRITING
COPPER CANYON PRESS TITLES,
PLEASE CALL 360-385-4925 EXT. 103

WE ARE GRATEFUL FOR THE MAJOR SUPPORT PROVIDED BY:

Anonymous

Richard Andrews and
    Colleen Chartier

Jill Baker and Jeffrey Bishop

Anne and Geoffrey Barker

Donna Bellew

Will Blythe

John Branch

Diana Broze

John R. Cahill

Sarah Cavanaugh

Keith Cowan and Linda Walsh

Peter Currie

Stephanie Ellis-Smith and
    Douglas Smith

Mimi Gardner Gates

Gull Industries Inc.
    on behalf of William True

Carolyn and Robert Hedin

David and Jane Hibbard

Bruce S. Kahn

Phil Kovacevich and Eric Wechsler

Maureen Lee and Mark Busto

Ellie Mathews and Carl Youngmann
    as The North Press

Larry Mawby and Lois Bahle

Petunia Charitable Fund and
    adviser Elizabeth Hebert

Suzanne Rapp and Mark Hamilton

Adam and Lynn Rauch

Emily and Dan Raymond

Joseph C. Roberts

Cynthia Sears

Kim and Jeff Seely

Tree Swenson

Barbara and Charles Wright

In honor of C.D. Wright,
    from Forrest Gander

Caleb Young as C. Young Creative

The dedicated interns and faithful
    volunteers of Copper Canyon Press

The pressmark for Copper Canyon Press
suggests entrance, connection, and interaction
while holding at its center
an attentive, dynamic space for poetry.

This book is set in FF Good Pro and Adobe Text Pro.
Cover design by Becca Fox Design.
Book design by Claretta Holsey.
Printed on archival-quality paper.